FlashRevise Pocketbook

AS/A-Level Sociology

Crime & Deviance with Theory & Method

Philip Allan Updates, an imprint of Hodder Education, an Hachette UK company, Market Place, Deddington, Oxfordshire OX15 0SE

Orders

Bookpoint Ltd, 130 Milton Park, Abingdon, Oxfordshire OX14 4SB
tel: 01235 827720 fax: 01235 400454 e-mail: uk.orders@bookpoint.co.uk

Lines are open 9.00 a.m.–5.00 p.m., Monday to Saturday, with a 24-hour message answering service. You can also order through our website: www.philipallan.co.uk

ISBN 978-1-4441-0263-5

Impression number 5 4 3 2 1
Year 2015 2014 2013 2012 2011 2010

Printed in Spain

P01664

Crime and deviance

1 The official criminal statistics
2 Recording crime
3 Reporting crime
4 Victim surveys
5 Policing
6 Sociological perspectives on criminal statistics
7 Durkheim and functionalism (1)
8 Durkheim and functionalism (2)
9 Durkheim and functionalism (3)
10 Merton and functionalism (1)
11 Merton and functionalism (2)
12 Merton and functionalism (3)
13 Merton and functionalism (4)
14 Merton and functionalism (5)
15 Subcultural theory (1)
16 Subcultural theory (2)
17 Subcultural theory (3)
18 Subcultural theory (4)
19 Subcultural theory (5)
20 Subcultural theory (6)
21 Ecological theory
22 Labelling theory (1)
23 Labelling theory (2)
24 Labelling theory (3)
25 Labelling theory (4)
26 Moral panic theory (1)
27 Moral panic theory (2)
28 Marxism (1)
29 Marxism (2)
30 Marxism (3)
31 Global and environmental crime
32 Neo-Marxism (1)
33 Neo-Marxism (2)
34 Right realism (1)
35 Right realism (2)
36 Right realism (3)
37 Right realism (4)
38 Right realism (5)
39 Left realism (1)
40 Left realism (2)
41 Gender and crime (1)
42 Gender and crime (2)
43 Gender and crime (3)
44 Ethnicity and crime (1)
45 Ethnicity and crime (2)
46 Suicide (1)
47 Suicide (2)
48 Suicide (3)
49 Suicide (4)
50 Suicide (5)
51 Suicide (6)
52 Suicide (7)

The official criminal statistics

Q1 Approximately what percentage of total recorded crime in 2008 was violent crime?

Q2 What, according to the official criminal statistics, is the social profile of the typical offender in terms of age, social class, gender and ethnicity?

Q3 What is the dark figure of crime?

Q4 What do interpretivists mean when they say that the official crime statistics are socially constructed?

ANSWERS

A1 22%.

A2 The typical criminal is likely to be male, aged between 15 and 21, working class and possibly black in some inner city areas.

A3 Crime that is either unreported and undetected.

A4 Crime statistics are the end product of a complex process of collection and may tell us more about those involved in that collection than about crime and criminals.

examiner's note Positivists believe that the criminal statistics are collected in a reliable and scientific fashion. Interpretivists believe they do not give us a valid picture of crime and criminals because of the way in which such statistics are collected.

Recording crime

Q1 What detected crimes are not included in the official criminal statistics?

Q2 What is a self-report study?

Q3 Why do the findings of self-report studies call into question the accuracy of the official criminal statistics?

Q4 Identify three methodological problems that call into question the value of self-reports.

ANSWERS

A1 Those dealt with by non-police agencies such as the Inland Revenue, Customs and Excise and the armed services.

A2 An anonymous self-completion questionnaire, in which people admit to unreported and undetected crime.

A3 Such studies suggest that crime rates should be higher and that more middle-class people and women commit crime than the official statistics indicate.

A4
- Validity — people, especially boys and young men, lie and exaggerate
- Representativeness — most surveys over-focus on young people because they are easier to access than criminals
- Relevance — most crime uncovered tends to be trivial

examiner's note Official criminal statistics are a type of secondary data and, although they are cheap and easy to access, their secondhand nature can undermine their validity and usefulness to sociologists.

Reporting crime

Q1 Identify three reasons why the increased affluence of society may have contributed to a rise in the official criminal statistics.

Q2 In what ways might the rise in violent crime be linked to changes in social attitudes?

Q3 What is a victimless crime?

Q4 Why might crimes committed against children or the elderly be under-reported?

ANSWERS

A1 • There is more property, particularly consumer items, to steal, e.g. mobile phones
• Tolerance of property crime has decreased as society has become more property-centred
• People are more likely to have insurance

A2 People may be more intolerant of violent crime and consequently more willing to report it. For example, women today may no longer be willing to put up with domestic violence.

A3 Victimless crime often involves two offenders, e.g. a prostitute/client or a drug pusher/user.

A4 They may not realise a crime has been committed against them.

examiner's note Crime statistics may tell us more about the attitudes of the general public and victims of crime than they tell us about crime and criminals.

Victim surveys

Q1 What is the British Crime Survey (BCS)?

Q2 How do the findings of the BCS compare with the official crime statistics?

Q3 Give three reasons why the reliability of the BCS can be questioned.

Q4 What do more localised crime surveys such as the Islington and Merseyside crime surveys indicate?

A1 A government survey involving approximately 40,000 people, asking if they have been victims of crime and have reported that crime to the police.

A2 People regard many crimes as too trivial to report or have little faith in the police.

A3 People's recollections are often faulty or biased; people may not be aware a crime has been committed against them; the BCS does not include certain categories of crimes, e.g. white collar and corporate crime.

A4 They suggest that the chance of being a victim of crime in some inner city areas is very high, particularly for ethnic minorities and the poor. Such groups are also often subject to repeat victimisation.

examiner's note Be aware of the methodology of victim surveys and how the employment of questionnaires, laptop computers and unstructured interviews conducted by female researchers can affect the validity of the data collected.

Policing

Q1 Identify three reasons why 57% of all crimes reported to the police fail to appear in the criminal statistics.

Q2 How might police discretion on the streets bias the criminal statistics?

Q3 What did the McPherson Report conclude about policing in London?

Q4 How might policing bias the official criminal statistics?

A1 The police may:

- regard the offence as too trivial to record
- classify it as less serious in order to manipulate statistics so that they appear more efficient
- view the social status of the person doing the reporting as not high enough to pursue the issue

A2 Police officers may use stereotypical assumptions about criminal or suspicious behaviour and consequently stop, search and arrest members of some groups rather than others.

A3 It concluded that the London police were institutionally racist with the result that black and Asian people receive more negative attention from police officers.

A4 Some groups may appear more in the criminal statistics because of biased policing rather than because they are more criminal.

examiner's note Examine research that looks at the occupational culture of the British police to assess how the attitudes and behaviour of police officers can affect the criminal statistics.

Sociological perspectives on criminal statistics

Q1 How do Marxist sociologists generally regard criminal statistics?

Q2 What do left realists think of the interpretivist view that the official statistics are socially constructed?

Q3 Why are feminist sociologists generally critical of the official criminal statistics?

Q4 What is the postmodernist attitude towards the official criminal statistics?

ANSWERS

A1 Crime statistics function to reflect the view that the law supports the interests of the ruling class. The statistics aim to scapegoat and criminalise the working class.

A2 The interpretivist critique is exaggerated and the working class does commit most crime, mainly against working-class victims.

A3 Feminists believe that crimes against women, such as rape and domestic violence, are not truly reflected in the criminal statistics.

A4 The collection of statistics is no longer geared to catching criminals but rather to informing people how best to avoid becoming victims of crime.

***examiner's* note** The debate about crime statistics is essentially a debate about the reliability and validity of secondary data. The debate regarding suicide is very similar.

Durkheim and functionalism (1)

Q1 Identify two positive functions of crime, according to Durkheim.

Q2 What extreme form of deviance did Durkheim study to illustrate the influence of society on individual behaviour?

Q3 Durkheim warned of the dangers of too much and too little crime in society. What were these dangers?

Q4 What did Durkheim mean when he said 'yesterday's deviance must become today's normality'?

ANSWERS

A1 • Public outrage promotes consensus, e.g. 9/11
• Crime reinforces value consensus by reminding society of the difference between 'right' and 'wrong'

A2 Suicide.

A3 • Too much crime can be dangerous and can lead to social disintegration
• Too little crime may indicate a repressive society, e.g. a totalitarian dictatorship

A4 Behaviour seen as deviant in the past draws society's attention to matters that might need changing, such as anomalies in the law or the organisation of society.

***examiner's* note** Durkheim's theory is not really an explanation of why people commit crime — it is an explanation of social control.

Durkheim and functionalism (2)

Q1 What type of social control agency are institutions such as the family, the peer group and religion?

Q2 Give two examples of formal agencies of social control.

Q3 What did Durkheim mean by the concept of anomie?

Q4 How might anomie lead to crime and deviance in modern societies?

A1 Informal agencies.

A2 Any two from: the law, the police and the judiciary.

A3 Moral confusion, i.e. a state of normlessness.

A4 People unsure about moral standards or constraints may not be as committed as the rest of the community to rules, laws etc.

examiner's note Durkheim's analysis of crime and deviance is too positive for some sociologists because he does not really discuss the negative effects of such behaviour.

Durkheim and functionalism (3)

Q1 Why might Durkheim's ideas about crime be criticised by victim support groups?

Q2 Why are Marxist sociologists critical of Durkheim's view that crime functions for the good of the whole community?

Q3 What evidence is there that crime can destroy communities or isolate individuals, rather than reinforce community and value consensus?

Q4 Why are interpretivists critical of the concept of anomie?

ANSWERS

A1 Crime often has a severe or dysfunctional effect rather than a positive one, on individuals, families and communities.

A2 The powerful may whip up community concerns about crime in support of their own interests or manipulate such concerns to divert attention from inequalities created by their policies.

A3 Fear of crime leads to people, especially the elderly and women, retreating from society by not going out at night, not talking to strangers etc.

A4 Anomie is difficult to operationalise and therefore difficult to observe and measure.

examiner's note Durkheim was the first sociologist to suggest that the causes of crime and deviance were structural rather than originating in individual deficiencies.

Merton and functionalism (1)

Q1 What is the 'American Dream' on which the functionalist Robert Merton focuses his theory of crime and deviance?

Q2 What is the main goal of Western capitalist societies, according to Merton?

Q3 What means are available in capitalist society to achieve this goal?

Q4 What causes crime and deviance, according to Merton?

ANSWERS

A1 The 'American Dream' refers to an idealistic set of beliefs that suggest the USA provides equal opportunities for all, regardless of social background, to be economically successful.

A2 Material wealth.

A3 Education and employment.

A4 Strain between the social goals and the legitimate means of achieving those goals.

***examiner's* note** Like Durkheim, Merton is a structuralist who sees the causes of crime and deviance originating in the social organisation of society.

Merton and functionalism (2)

Q1 What is anomie, according to Merton?

Q2 What types of factor are likely to block opportunities?

Q3 Which social groups are more likely to experience anomie?

Q4 Why can Merton's theory be described as a structural theory of crime?

ANSWERS

A1 The frustration (strain) that results from being unable to achieve social goals.

A2 Strain can be caused by racism, patriarchy, ascription, nepotism, minority monopoly of wealth and power etc.

A3 Those at the bottom of the socioeconomic hierarchy, e.g. the working class, the poor and minority ethnic groups.

A4 Because crime and deviance originate in the social processes that set social goals (e.g. culture) and that create the social institutions (e.g. education and the economy), which fail to provide the means to achieve those goals.

examiner's note Examiners often ask candidates to contrast functionalist theories with other structuralist theories such as Marxism.

Merton and functionalism (3)

Q1 How do most people respond to the strain between goals and means?

Q2 Which response to strain involves an acceptance of the social goals but a rejection of legitimate means?

Q3 Which adaptation rejects both the social goals and the means of achieving those goals?

Q4 What is the relationship of rebels to the social goals and the conventional means of achieving them?

ANSWERS

A1 They conform to social norms.

A2 Innovation (e.g. crime).

A3 Retreatism (e.g. dropping out of college).

A4 They attempt to replace them with a set of their own.

examiner's note Be evaluative. For example, note that Merton fails to explain why individuals choose particular responses, i.e. why most conform rather than innovate, or why some retreat rather than rebel.

Merton and functionalism (4)

Q1 Which of Merton's responses to strain involves losing sight of social goals but a blind acceptance of the means of achieving them?

Q2 Which adaptation is likely to lead to responses such as alcoholism, drug-taking and suicide?

Q3 Which of Merton's five potential responses to strain are deviant in their behaviour?

Q4 In what sense is the criminal similar to the law-abiding citizen, according to Merton?

ANSWERS

A1 Ritualism.

A2 Retreatism.

A3 Innovation, retreatism and rebellion.

A4 The criminal or innovator subscribes to the same set of cultural goals, e.g. material success, as other members of society.

***examiner's* note** Merton has produced a critique of capitalist society that is similar to that produced by Marxists such as David Gordon. It is important to realise that, despite their differences, there are similarities between the functionalist and Marxist theories of society.

Merton and functionalism (5)

Q1 What types of non-economic crime does Merton fail to explain?

Q2 What type of crime committed by people of high status does Merton fail to explain?

Q3 Why are Marxists critical of Merton's acceptance that the law treats everybody equally?

Q4 Which British sociologist has adapted Merton's ideas to explain why African-Caribbean youth commits crime?

ANSWERS

A1 Violence, sexual offences and juvenile delinquency, such as vandalism and gang crime. These crimes are not motivated by monetary gain.

A2 White-collar and corporate crime.

A3 Merton fails to ask 'who benefits from the making of laws?' Marxists argue that the ruling class does.

A4 Cashmore.

***examiner's* note** Merton's concept of anomie is influential and is implied in sociological explanations that link crime to social and economic disadvantage, such as left realism.

Subcultural theory (1)

Q1 What is meant by the concept of subculture?

Q2 What type of crime does subcultural theory focus on?

Q3 What is the central goal that young people attempt to attain in modern societies, according to Albert Cohen?

Q4 Why are working-class boys more likely to fail at school, according to Cohen?

ANSWERS

A1 A social group that supports norms and values that are different from mainstream culture.

A2 Juvenile delinquency.

A3 Status: feelings of self-worth or esteem, both in the eyes of others and in the individual.

A4 Parents fail to equip them with the necessary skills.

***examiner's* note** The concept of subculture is central to a variety of sociological theories of crime and deviance, including labelling theory, Marxism and left realism.

Subcultural theory (2)

Q1 Why does Cohen blame education as well as parents for working-class delinquency?

Q2 What concept does Cohen suggest to explain the disaffection of working-class boys?

Q3 How do they compensate for the disaffection they feel?

Q4 What alternative sociological term can be used for delinquent subcultures that reverse social norms and values?

ANSWERS

A1 Schools deny working-class children status by placing them in bottom streams/sets and labelling them as failures.

A2 Status frustration.

A3 They form anti-school subcultures and award status to each other on the basis of anti-school and delinquent activities.

A4 Counter-cultures.

examiner's note Be aware that, when sociologists talk about the delinquent activities of working-class boys, they are talking about only a minority of such boys. A weakness of subcultural theories is that they fail to explain why the majority of working-class boys generally conform.

Subcultural theory (3)

Q1 How might you use Paul Willis's study of working-class lads to criticise Cohen's ideas?

Q2 What criticism might be made of the way Cohen views working-class parenting?

Q3 What role do working-class girls play in Cohen's analysis?

Q4 How might the concept of 'drift' be used to criticise subcultural theory?

ANSWERS

A1 Willis's lads chose to fail and to engage in delinquent activities because they saw qualifications as irrelevant to their futures, rather than because they had experienced status frustration.

A2 His view suggests that all working-class parenting is inadequate.

A3 He ignores working-class girls altogether.

A4 Young people often drift between conformity and deviance, and are not committed to delinquency as a way of life.

***examiner's* note** Cohen's theory is typical of malestream sociology, i.e. sociological studies that assume females are less criminal than males.

Subcultural theory (4)

Q1 How does Walter Miller view lower-class culture?

Q2 Why do lower-class youth engage in crime, according to Miller?

Q3 Give three examples of the focal concerns that lead to juvenile delinquency, according to Miller's theory.

Q4 What ethnographic research technique did Parker use to study the subculture of working-class boys in Liverpool in the 1960s?

ANSWERS

A1 It is naturally 'deviant', in that it subscribes to values and norms that are likely to lead to confrontation with mainstream middle-class society.

A2 To compensate for the boredom of the working-class experience of school and work.

A3 Any three from: toughness and aggression; looking for excitement; being streetwise; a heightened sense of masculinity; autonomy; fatalism etc.

A4 Participant observation.

examiner's note Miller's theory is pathological — it blames the cultural background of the delinquent (and by implication, the inadequate socialisation skills of lower-class parents).

Subcultural theory (5)

Q1 What does Matza mean when he criticises subcultural theory for over-predicting delinquency?

Q2 What are subterranean values and who subscribes to them?

Q3 Why is labelling theory critical of subcultural theory?

Q4 What is meant by the 'paradox of inclusion'?

A1 It implies that *all* working-class youth is delinquent whereas in reality only a small minority is.

A2 Values such as the need or search for excitement or to be outrageous, and most people subscribe to them.

A3 Powerless groups such as the working class and ethnic minorities are more likely to be negatively labelled as criminal or deviant for behaviour that most groups engage in.

A4 Black youths are excluded from society, but over-compensate by identifying themselves with consumer culture through the acquisition of high-status material goods and brands.

examiner's note Labelling theory is an interpretivist theory, which examiners often contrast with structuralist theories.

Subcultural theory (6)

Q1 Why do postmodernists reject subcultural theory?

Q2 What do postmodernists mean when they say crime is 'seductive'?

Q3 What does Lyng mean when he describes delinquency as 'edgework'?

Q4 Why are feminists often critical of subcultural theories of delinquency?

A1 Subcultural theory suggests delinquency is a rational response to social circumstances. Postmodernists suggest delinquency is an irrational behaviour.

A2 Young males quite simply get involved in delinquency because it is thrilling.

A3 Delinquency involves danger and risk — going to the edge of acceptable behaviour.

A4 Subcultural theory generally ignores female delinquency.

***examiner's* note** Postmodern theory is critical of most conventional theories of crime and delinquency.

Ecological theory

Q1 How are cities organised, according to the Chicago School sociologists Shaw and McKay?

Q2 Which area of the city often has the highest crime rates?

Q3 What is social disorganisation?

Q4 What is cultural transmission theory?

ANSWERS

A1 Into distinct neighbourhoods or zones with their own values and lifestyles, e.g. business areas, inner cities, suburbs etc.

A2 Zone 2, also known as the zone of transmission or inner city, where rates of migration, divorce, poor housing, unemployment etc. are high.

A3 Lack of informal social controls — there is little sense of community or of duty and obligation to neighbours and, therefore, fewer barriers to crime.

A4 The view that crime is culturally acceptable among the poorest groups living in inner city areas who socialise their children into deviant patterns of behaviour.

examiner's note The cultural transmission theory of Shaw and McKay has strongly influenced Charles Murray's underclass theory.

Labelling theory (1)

Q1 What is the alternative name for labelling theory?

Q2 What does labelling theory mean when it argues that 'normality' and 'deviance' are relative concepts?

Q3 How might a deviant act such as killing a person be viewed as a matter of interpretation?

Q4 Labelling theory argues that deviance involves two activities. What do interactionists mean by this?

ANSWERS

A1 Symbolic interactionism.

A2 Definitions of what constitutes 'right' or 'wrong' behaviour differ according to historical period, culture, subculture and specific social context.

A3 Killing people may be justifiable if done in the context of self-defence, or if carried out by soldiers in times of war or police officers in the course of duty.

A4 A group or individual must act in a particular way and another, more powerful, group or individual must label that activity as deviant.

examiner's note Labelling theory focuses on the relationship between deviance and power. It is interpretivist: it examines interaction and the social meanings that people attach to deviant actions.

Labelling theory (2)

Q1 What is primary deviance?

Q2 What is secondary deviance?

Q3 Who are the agents who allegedly socially control behaviour on behalf of the powerful by labelling the activities of the less powerful as deviant?

Q4 Why might young blacks appear more in the criminal statistics than young whites, according to labelling theory?

ANSWERS

A1 The initial rule-breaking.

A2 The reaction of the person labelled as a criminal or deviant, which usually has a greater social consequence than the initial deviant act.

A3 The police, judiciary, social workers, teachers, politicians, journalists etc.

A4 Because the police label them as more suspicious and criminal, and consequently stop them more than other social groups.

examiner's note Sociologists influenced by labelling theory have produced a substantive critique of the official criminal statistics by examining police–suspect interaction and the occupational culture of the police.

Labelling theory (3)

Q1 What is a master status?

Q2 What negative effects can the master status have for labelled individuals?

Q3 How have interactionists used the concept of the self-fulfilling prophecy to explain crime and deviance?

Q4 How might a master status lead to subcultural responses in those labelled as deviant or criminal?

ANSWERS

A1 A status that overrides all other statuses in a person's life, e.g. ex-convict, sex offender.

A2 Society interprets all actions and motives in the context of that label, making it extremely difficult for the 'deviant' to integrate into 'normal' society.

A3 A criminal label can lead to re-offending because it undermines trust and the resumption of a normal routine, e.g. getting a job.

A4 The 'deviant' may seek solace, comfort, sympathy and normality in the company of others similarly labelled.

examiner's note This approach to crime and deviance is similar to how labelling theory explains success and failure in the educational system.

Labelling theory (4)

Q1 In what way is the concept of the self-fulfilling prophecy over-deterministic?

Q2 In what way is the process of being labelled open to 'negotiation'?

Q3 Which criminal activities are always more important than the societal reaction, according to Akers?

Q4 Why are Marxists critical of the interactionist use of the concept of power?

ANSWERS

A1 It implies that a deviant label automatically leads to further acts of deviance.

A2 Some groups or individuals can choose to reject or resist deviant labels.

A3 Murder, rape, child abuse etc. are not dependent on a societal reaction — they are quite simply wrong.

A4 Labelling theorists are vague about who wields power. Marxists suggest it is the capitalist class.

examiner's note Interactionism has illustrated the complexity of defining deviance, the role of power differences and the consequences of being negatively labelled.

Moral panic theory (1)

Q1 What is meant by a moral panic?

Q2 Which general theory does moral panic theory derive from?

Q3 What is a folk devil?

Q4 What is a moral entrepreneur?

ANSWERS

A1 Social anxiety, disproportionate to the real threat offered, caused by sensationalist and stereotyped news reporting.

A2 Interactionism or labelling theory.

A3 Any social group demonised by the media, stereotyped and presented as a threat to society, about which 'something must be done', e.g. youth cultures.

A4 Any prominent social commentator who influences and shapes public opinion during moral panics.

***examiner's* note** This debate suggests that media content can influence the attitudes and behaviour of the general public. Critics note that this is impossible to prove methodologically.

Moral panic theory (2)

Q1 What is the cause of moral panics, according to Stan Cohen?

Q2 What is the cause of moral panics, according to Marxists?

Q3 What is deviancy amplification?

Q4 Identify three possible consequences of a moral panic?

ANSWERS

A1 • A lack of newsworthy events
• Social and economic change

A2 Crises of capitalism caused by economic mismanagement.

A3 The initial deviance is simply made worse by the moral panic — a minor or fantasy problem is sensationalised and transformed into a real problem.

A4 • Changes in the law
• More policing
• Subcultural response in the form of further deviance
• Rise in the crime statistics

***examiner's* note** It is advisable to be able to describe the stages of a moral panic in detail using a contemporary example.

Marxism (1)

Q1 According to Gordon, what inequalities caused by the capitalist system generate crime?

Q2 What dominant values in capitalist society encourage all social classes to commit crime, according to Gordon?

Q3 How might lack of job satisfaction or power at work result in crime, according to Marxists?

Q4 What is the key question David Gordon asks about working-class crime?

ANSWERS

A1 Poverty, homelessness, unemployment, low pay, class inequalities in the distribution of wealth etc.

A2 Competition, materialism, individualism and greed.

A3 Some workers may feel so alienated and frustrated that they turn to crime in order to compensate.

A4 Why working-class people do not commit more crime.

***examiner's* note** Marxism, like functionalism, is a structuralist theory — Gordon blames the organisation of capitalist society for crime.

Marxism (2)

Q1 What are the major priorities of capitalism protected by the law, according to Mannheim?

Q2 How does Althusser view the law?

Q3 According to Marxists, the law works in the interests of which group?

Q4 What do Marxists mean when they say the law is enforced 'selectively'?

ANSWERS

A1 Wealth, private property and profit.

A2 As an ideology — a set of rules aimed primarily at protecting the interests of the wealthy.

A3 The ruling class.

A4 Working-class people are policed more heavily than the middle class or ruling class.

examiner's note The Marxist theory of crime and deviance sees the law functioning socially to control the working class. It is empirically difficult to prove that laws benefit one particular class.

Marxism (3)

Q1 What do sociologists call the type of crime that is committed by middle-class individuals abusing their occupational role?

Q2 What is corporate crime?

Q3 What did Stephen Box mean when he said that 'the powerful engage in a process of mystification in regard to corporate crime'?

Q4 Identify four characteristics of corporate crime that contribute to its underestimation in the official criminal statistics.

A1 White-collar crime.

A2 Crime committed by companies or corporations as a result of deliberate decisions made by high-ranking executives and managers.

A3 They have influenced the general public into believing that corporate crime is less serious and harmful than conventional crime.

A4 Invisible; complex; morally ambiguous; indirect in its victimisation; perceived as less threatening and therefore less serious.

***examiner's* note** Detailed knowledge of this type of crime is an excellent way to illustrate Marxist ideas.

Global and environmental crime

Q1 Give examples of the types of crime that have increased because of globalisation.

Q2 What is transnational crime?

Q3 Give examples of environmental or green crimes.

Q4 What is state crime? Give examples.

ANSWERS

A1 Trafficking in drugs, weapons and human beings; corruption, terrorism and war crimes.

A2 Crime committed by global corporations, especially tax evasion, insider trading, exploitation of employment laws, dumping toxic waste etc.

A3 Crimes committed against the environment include air and water pollution and the dumping of hazardous waste.

A4 Crimes such as torture and ethnic cleansing, committed by politicians, civil servants, members of the armed services and security services on behalf of particular governments.

examiner's note Note that corporate crime, global crime, state crime and green crime are all inter-related.

Neo-Marxism (1)

Q1 Which sociologists are associated with the neo-Marxist or new criminological theory of crime and deviance?

Q2 What do the neo-Marxist criminologists mean when they say working-class crime is 'political'?

Q3 According to this theory, what is the political motive behind crimes such as burglary, robbery and theft?

Q4 What is the main criticism directed at the idea that burglary and robbery are political crimes?

A1 Taylor, Walton and Young.

A2 They see crime as a form of protest against the class inequality, injustice and exploitation characteristic of modern capitalism.

A3 An attempt to redistribute wealth from rich to poor.

A4 Most victims of burglary and robbery are working class.

examiner's note Neo-Marxism is an interpretivist theory because it suggests that crime is a reaction to how people interpret the social world around them. Unfortunately there has been little research on how criminals interpret their activities.

Neo-Marxism (2)

Q1 How does Paul Gilroy explain crime committed by young African-Caribbeans?

Q2 What crime does Stuart Hall argue resulted in a moral panic in the early 1970s, which divided the working class along racial lines?

Q3 What is a crisis of hegemony?

Q4 How does the ruling class attempt to divert society's attention from crises of hegemony, according to Hall?

A1 It is a reflection of young black people's anger at slavery, colonialism and their perception that the police persecute them.

A2 Mugging.

A3 A challenge to the cultural domination of the ruling class, especially its ability to manage the economy effectively, caused by recession, unemployment, inflation and union militancy.

A4 By encouraging moral panics in the media that scapegoat powerless groups.

***examiner's* note** This theory is probably too conspiratorial — it is difficult, if not impossible, to uncover evidence of deliberate collusion between the ruling class, the police and mass media.

Right realism (1)

Q1 Which political or philosophical position is right realism most closely associated with?

Q2 Why do people commit crime, according to right realists?

Q3 What is the right realist attitude towards the treatment of criminals by the police and the state?

Q4 What is the right realist attitude towards policing?

ANSWERS

A1 Conservative or new-right thinking.

A2 Right realists see human beings as naturally selfish, individualistic and greedy — it is part of their nature to commit crime.

A3 Punishment, particularly prison, is too soft — the rate of re-offending suggests that it needs to be harsher.

A4 The police have failed to prevent and reduce crime.

***examiner's* note** This view of crime became influential during the 1980s and 1990s — a period in which there was a substantial rise in crime.

Right realism (2)

Q1 What do right realists mean when they claim that informal community controls have broken down?

Q2 What does Travis Hirschi mean when he notes that most crime is opportunistic?

Q3 What does Hirschi mean when he claims that the benefits of crime generally outweigh the costs?

Q4 What does Hirschi recommend so that potential criminals rationally decide not to commit crime?

ANSWERS

A1 The informal controls and responsibilities encouraged by parents, neighbours and peer groups have weakened.

A2 Most people would commit crime if the opportunity presented itself and they stood little chance of being caught.

A3 The costs of crime, i.e. the chances of being caught or severely punished, are outweighed by the benefits, i.e. the chances of getting away with it.

A4 That the costs of crime clearly outweigh the benefits.

examiner's note Hirschi is generally critical of the overall criminal justice system, which he sees as weak and ineffective.

Right realism (3)

Q1 Identify the four controls that exist in most people's lives that result in the costs of crime clearly outweighing the benefits.

Q2 Why are young people more likely to commit crime, according to Hirschi?

Q3 Which deviant subculture, allegedly found in inner city areas, is also likely to lack these controls, according to Charles Murray?

Q4 Which type of 'deviant' family set-up is alleged by Murray to be found in this subculture?

ANSWERS

A1 Attachment to family; commitment to education and career; involvement in community; belief in law and respect for others.

A2 They are less likely to have these controls in their lives until they are older.

A3 The underclass.

A4 Single-parent families, mainly headed by single mothers.

***examiner's* note** The concept of a deviant underclass scapegoats the poor as being responsible for their situation.

Right realism (4)

Q1 What does Murray mean when he describes the underclass as 'welfare-dependent'?

Q2 Why is Murray critical of the way children are socialised in the underclass?

Q3 What is the attitude of the underclass towards the police and authority in general, according to Murray?

Q4 Why are Rex and Tomlinson critical of the concept of the underclass?

ANSWERS

A1 Members of the underclass allegedly choose to live off state benefits.

A2 Single mothers allegedly have no control over their delinquent children and, consequently, such children are often socialised into criminal and immoral behaviour.

A3 It is hostile.

A4 Most poverty is caused by factors beyond the control of the individual, e.g. recession, and evidence suggests that the poor do not generally subscribe to deviant values.

examiner's note The underclass theory is a pathological theory in that it firmly blames individual shortcomings for crime and poverty. However there is no convincing evidence that an underclass as a distinctive subculture exists in the UK.

Right realism (5)

Q1 What do right realists mean when they say victims should 'design out' crime?

Q2 What is meant by the term 'zero-tolerance policing'?

Q3 What do right realists recommend in terms of punishment for crime?

Q4 What is the right realist attitude towards surveillance?

ANSWERS

A1 They mean that victims need to take more responsibility for reducing crime by making themselves harder targets, by investing in more security, surveillance etc.

A2 That the police should not tolerate either serious or trivial crime, and that all offenders should be arrested and punished.

A3 Punishment should be made more severe, e.g. 'three strikes and you're out', which, in California means life imprisonment.

A4 There should be more CCTV in order to deter criminals.

***examiner's* note** These solutions to crime became popular in the USA and the UK in the 1990s. Be aware that the Labour government's attempts to clamp down on antisocial behaviour, e.g. through ASBOs, are influenced by right realist approaches.

Left realism (1)

Q1 What did Young and Lea's Islington Crime Survey of victims of crime conclude?

Q2 What do Young and Lea conclude about the official criminal statistics?

Q3 How do Young and Lea view white-collar crime compared with working-class crime?

Q4 What is Young and Lea's attitude towards poverty as a cause of crime?

ANSWERS

A1 That working-class people and black people, especially females and the elderly, are more at risk of being victims of crime than other groups.

A2 The statistics are generally correct in showing that working-class youth commits more crime than other social groups.

A3 It is as important but they note that people feel more threatened by the street crime found in inner city neighbourhoods.

A4 It is too simplistic to see poverty as responsible for crime; they blame relative deprivation and marginalisation.

examiner's note Left realists argue that other theories of crime and deviance are unrealistic about the causes of crime.

Left realism (2)

Q1 Left realists focus on intra-class and intra-ethnic crimes. What is meant by these terms?

Q2 How does the concept of relative deprivation help explain youth crime?

Q3 What role does the concept of marginalisation play in the decision to turn to crime?

Q4 According to left realism, what kinds of group commonly form as a result of relative deprivation and marginalisation?

A1 Crimes committed by members of one social class or ethnic group against each other.

A2 White and black working-class youngsters compare themselves with middle-class and white youth and feel deprived.

A3 People or groups who have been marginalised by society lack power, which may lead to disaffection — especially if their low status is reinforced by factors such as racism or over-policing.

A4 Subcultural, criminal or deviant gangs form in order to compensate for feelings of resentment generated by relative deprivation and marginalisation.

examiner's note The concepts of relative deprivation and marginalisation are similar to the political concept of 'social exclusion'. Left realists have also highlighted the effects of crime on victims — a group neglected by most theories of crime.

Gender and crime (1)

Q1 What percentage of those convicted of serious crimes such as violence is male?

Q2 How might the chivalry factor account for women being under-represented in the criminal statistics?

Q3 What did Campbell's self-report study tell us about female criminality?

Q4 For which crimes, according to feminists, are women punished more harshly by the courts than men?

ANSWERS

A1 Approximately 80%.

A2 This suggests that male police officers are paternalistic — they are less likely to see women as suspicious or criminal and are less likely to stop, arrest or charge them.

A3 That it is a great deal higher than is officially recorded.

A4 Murder of spouses or children.

***examiner's* note** Female crime, especially violent crime, has risen at a more rapid rate than male crime in the last 10 years.

Gender and crime (2)

Q1 What do feminist sociologists mean when they accuse theories of crime and deviance of being 'gender-blind'?

Q2 How might gender-role socialisation into masculine values and norms be responsible for the high male crime rate?

Q3 How might gender-role socialisation into feminine values and norms be responsible for female under-representation in crime statistics?

Q4 What social controls may operate in the family and society that limit opportunities for female crime?

ANSWERS

A1 Many sociological theories of crime have ignored females.

A2 Dominant masculine values may encourage criminal behaviour, e.g. toughness, aggression, risk-taking, dominance.

A3 Dominant feminine values include passive qualities such as caring, empathy, communication, conformity etc., which may prevent or reduce criminal behaviour.

A4 Stricter parental controls over contact with peers and boyfriends; greater restriction to the home, e.g. in role of mother; harsher social penalties for deviant behaviour, e.g. being labelled with a bad reputation.

***examiner's* note** When answering questions on gender and crime, it is important not to neglect how masculinity influences male crime.

Gender and crime (3)

Q1 Why is white-collar crime dominated by males?

Q2 What is the feminisation of poverty and how might this increase female crime rates?

Q3 What types of female crime may be motivated by poverty?

Q4 What type of crime is rapidly increasing among young working-class females?

ANSWERS

A1 Women are less likely to be in high-status jobs.

A2 Women are more likely to be in poverty than men because they are more likely to be in low-paid jobs, to be single parents or elderly. They are therefore more likely to feel deprived or marginalised and, consequently, disaffected.

A3 Shoplifting, prostitution and social security fraud.

A4 Crimes of violence.

examiner's note Some explanations of working-class crime, e.g. underclass theory, may be relevant to understanding both female delinquency and educational underachievement.

Ethnicity and crime (1)

Q1 Which ethnic minority group is over-represented in the official criminal statistics?

Q2 Which ethnic minority groups are under-represented in the official criminal statistics?

Q3 What did the McPherson Report conclude in regard to the policing of ethnic minorities?

Q4 What do left realists conclude about the level of ethnic minority crime found in the official criminal statistics?

A1 African-Caribbeans.

A2 Asians and Chinese.

A3 Institutional racism in the Metropolitan Police Force had led to the over-policing of the African-Caribbean community.

A4 That the statistics about crime by African-Caribbeans are correct, despite concerns about the over-policing of black people.

***examiner's* note** There are signs that levels of crime among young British-born Pakistanis and Bangladeshis are rising.

Ethnicity and crime (2)

Q1 How does Cashmore explain African-Caribbean street crime, using Merton's theory of anomie?

Q2 Why is black street crime political, according to Paul Gilroy?

Q3 What factors does Tony Sewell blame for street crime committed by young African-Caribbeans?

Q4 What causes black street crime, according to Charles Murray?

ANSWERS

A1 Many young African-Caribbeans have their opportunities blocked by racism, failing inner city schools and unemployment, and turn to crime as a form of innovation.

A2 Gilroy argues that black street crime is motivated by anger at slavery, colonialism and the everyday experience of racism, especially from the police.

A3 The lack of a father figure; the need to gain street credibility, status and respect, which motivates the need to prove one's masculinity; media culture's emphasis on consumerism, bling etc.

A4 Membership of the underclass.

***examiner's* note** Many explanations of working-class crime are relevant to explanations of ethnic minority crime. It is also important to remember that only a small minority of ethnic minority youth turns to crime — conformity is generally the norm.

Suicide (1)

Q1 Why did Durkheim choose to study suicide?

Q2 What scientific method did Durkheim use to study suicide?

Q3 What did Durkheim incorrectly assume about the official suicide statistics that he used?

Q4 What is meant by the suicide rate?

ANSWERS

A1 He was a positivist and wanted to prove that what most people saw as a highly individual act was actually caused by society.

A2 The comparative method, which involves comparing groups of statistics in order to find correlations.

A3 He assumed that the statistics had been collected in a standardised and scientific way across all societies.

A4 The suicide rate refers to the number of people who kill themselves in every 100,000 of the population.

examiner's note Durkheim intended to use the study of suicide to demonstrate the scientific or positivist nature of social enquiry.

Suicide (2)

Q1 What determines the suicide rate, according to Durkheim's hypothesis?

Q2 What does Durkheim mean by 'social integration'?

Q3 Name the three different types of suicide identified by Durkheim.

Q4 Which type of suicide was caused by 'excessive individualism'?

ANSWERS

A1 The degree of social integration and moral regulation in the population.

A2 A sense of belonging to society, i.e. community.

A3 Egoistic, altruistic and anomic.

A4 Egoistic.

examiner's note Egoistic suicide is the main type of suicide identified by Durkheim and is worth knowing about in detail.

Suicide (3)

Q1 Which religious system reduces excessive individualism, according to Durkheim?

Q2 What family characteristics are likely to increase the potential to commit suicide, according to Durkheim?

Q3 Which type of suicide is caused by people seeing society as more important than themselves?

Q4 Which type of suicide is more likely to be committed by prisoners?

A1 Catholicism, because it exerts strong community controls over its members.

A2 People who are single, separated or divorced are less likely to belong to family communities that exert controls over them.

A3 Altruistic.

A4 Fatalistic.

***examiner's* note** Durkheim can be criticised because it is unclear why people choose a particular suicidal action or how we are supposed to distinguish between types of suicide.

Suicide (4)

Q1 What did Halbwachs contribute to the positivist theory of suicide?

Q2 What, according to Douglas, does Durkheim ignore when examining national suicide rates?

Q3 How does Douglas explain apparently low suicide rates in Catholic societies?

Q4 What do interpretivists like Atkinson mean by criticising Durkheim for failing to see that suicide statistics are socially constructed?

ANSWERS

A1 He stated that suicide rates were higher in cities because urban areas suffered low levels of social integration.

A2 Durkheim ignores the cultural meanings that are attached to suicide in particular societies.

A3 Suicide rates are actually high, but because suicide is interpreted as a mortal sin, it is covered up, thus reducing the rates.

A4 Official statistics are the end result of a complex social process involving interaction between the victim, relatives, police officers and a legal official (the coroner) who labels the death as suicide.

examiner's note Douglas and Atkinson are interpretivists and are critical of Durkheim's methodology. They argue that he was too trusting of the scientific accuracy of the suicide statistics he used.

Suicide (5)

Q1 How did J. Maxwell Atkinson go about researching coroners?

Q2 What is a coroner?

Q3 What verdicts are available to English coroners?

Q4 What are the primary cues that coroners look for in order to suggest intent to die?

A1 He interviewed a number of coroners and observed inquests.

A2 A legal officer who investigates 'suspicious' deaths.

A3 Suicide, natural causes, homicide, misadventure and the open verdict.

A4 Suicide notes, the mode of death and the location of death.

***examiner's* note** Atkinson aimed to show that suicide rates tell us more about how particular societies go about investigating and recording death than about why people kill themselves.

Suicide (6)

Q1 Why are suicide notes generally not an effective tool for coroners to use in determining suicidal intent?

Q2 What secondary cues do coroners use when investigating possible suicides?

Q3 What problems do significant others, such as relatives and friends, cause when coroners attempt to investigate potential suicide?

Q4 Why does the 'open verdict' make it difficult to compare international rates of suicide?

ANSWERS

40% of those who commit suicide leave suicide notes; ...tes are destroyed by relatives and friends, and many are ...uous in meaning.

...spects of the victim's biography such as job loss, breakdown of long-term relationships, mental illness, health problems etc.

A3 They can influence the coroner's verdict by strongly presenting 'evidence' about the deceased's state of mind and behaviour immediately prior to death.

A4 This verdict, which is reserved for cases in which the evidence is ambiguous, does not exist in other countries.

examiner's note Coroners do not follow standardised rules — they apply their unique set of meanings and experiences to their investigation of suspicious death. Suicide rates may reflect individual coroners' decisions rather than levels of social integration etc.

Suicide (7)

Q1 What experiment did Atkinson conduct to illustrate his view that suicide statistics are socially constructed?

Q2 Which sociological approach argues that suicide rates are the product of structure?

Q3 Which sociological approach argues that suicide rates are the product of social action?

Q4 Whose study of suicide attempts to combine both social structure and social action?

A1 He asked Danish and English coroners to examine the same suspicious deaths and allocate verdicts to them, and compared the results. The Danish coroners were more likely to bring in suicide verdicts than the English coroners.

A2 Positivism.

A3 Interpretivism.

A4 Steve Taylor.

***examiner's* note** The combination of structure and action is known as 'structuration' and is associated with Giddens.

Modernist sociological theories

Q1 What is meant by 'modernism'?

Q2 What is a modernist sociological theory?

Q3 Give two examples of structuralist modernist theories.

Q4 Give two examples of a modernist theory focused on social action.

ANSWERS

A1 Modernism or modernity refers to a period of Western history, approximately 1800–2000, characterised by major technological, social and political advances.

A2 Modernist sociological theories aim to explain rationally why modern societies are organised in the way they are.

A3 Marxism and functionalism.

A4 Symbolic interactionism and labelling theory.

examiner's note Structuralist theories see the organisation (i.e. the structure) of society as more important than the individual, whereas social action theories see society as the result of interaction between individuals.

Functionalism (1)

Q1 In what way is functionalist theory underpinned by an organic analogy?

Q2 What is a functional prerequisite, according to Parsons?

Q3 What are the four prerequisites societies need to resolve in order to function effectively?

Q4 What does Parsons call the cultural choices of action available to members of society?

ANSWERS

A1 Society is compared to the human body. The organs of the body resemble social institutions such as the family, the educational system, the law etc. in the way that they all work together to ensure the overall health of the body and social system respectively.

A2 A basic need or function that must be fulfilled for society to survive.

A3
- To provide economically for members of society
- To make effective political decisions
- To bring about social integration and, consequently, social order and harmony
- To socialise members into shared beliefs and values

A4 Pattern variables.

examiner's note Be aware of Robert Merton's amendments to Parsons's functionalist theory of society.

Functionalism (2)

Q1 What is the difference between societies based on affectivity and those based on affective neutrality?

Q2 How does universalism differ from particularism?

Q3 What is the difference between self-orientation and collective orientation?

Q4 What is the difference between ascribed status and achieved status?

ANSWERS

A1 Societies based on affectivity are usually small scale because they are based on close loving or kinship-based relationships. Affective neutrality is normally found in large-scale societies in which relationships are based on neutral criteria such as rules, laws, qualifications, expertise etc.

A2 Universalism refers to the view that all individuals should be treated equally in terms of opportunities, i.e. judged on criteria such as examinations. Particularism refers to the preferential treatment that might be gained from belonging to a particular group, e.g. family, tribe, royalty.

A3 Self-orientation means putting individuality first whereas collective orientation means putting group interests before self-interest.

A4 Ascribed status is inherited and generally cannot be changed, e.g. gender. Achieved status is earned, e.g. qualifications.

***examiner's* note** Be able to illustrate the relationship between functional prerequisites and pattern variables.

Functionalism (3)

Q1 Why do functionalists believe that inequality is functional for society?

Q2 What do critics of functionalism mean when they argue that some social institutions can be 'dysfunctional' for society?

Q3 Why are interactionists critical of functionalism?

Q4 Why are Marxists critical of the functionalist idea that societies are characterised by consensus and order?

ANSWERS

A1 Functionalists believe modern societies such as the UK are meritocratic, therefore, those who reach the top deserve their superior rewards because they put in more effort or have more ability.

A2 Some institutions, e.g. religion, can bring societies together but can also drive societies apart.

A3 They accuse functionalists of viewing people as the 'puppets of society' and failing to see that people construct 'society' by coming together in social groups and making choices about action.

A4 They accuse functionalists of over-emphasising consensus and ignoring class conflict and differences in power.

examiner's note The major critique of functionalism is provided by Marxists and interactionists.

Marxism (1)

Q1 Of which economic system was Marx mainly critical?

Q2 What did Marx mean by the mode of production?

Q3 What factors constitute the means of production?

Q4 What did Marx call the relationship between those who owned the means of production and the working class?

A1 Capitalism.

A2 The dominant production process of the historical period — in modern societies this is industrial manufacturing, mainly carried out in factories.

A3 Capital (i.e. money), land, factories, technology and raw materials.

A4 The social relations of production.

***examiner's* note** Examiners are impressed with the accurate use of technical terms and concepts.

Marxism (2)

Q1 Which powerful group owns the means of production?

Q2 What alternative term does Marx use for the working class?

Q3 What characterises the social relations of production, according to Marx?

Q4 What are the majority of the working class suffering from, according to Marx?

ANSWERS

A1 Bourgeoisie (sometimes known as the capitalist class and the ruling class).

A2 Proletariat.

A3 Exploitation, class conflict and class inequality.

A4 False class consciousness.

examiner's note Be able to apply the Marxist economic model to modern capitalism.

Marxism (3)

Q1 What is the infrastructure?

Q2 What is the superstructure and how does it relate to the infrastructure?

Q3 What is ideology?

Q4 What is mass culture?

ANSWERS

A1 The economic system, i.e. capitalism.

A2 The superstructure is made up of social institutions such as the family, education system, religion, mass media, law. It operates to reproduce and legitimate the class inequality that exists in the infrastructure.

A3 Ideology refers to dominant ideas and values that exist and are accepted as 'normal' and 'natural'. These are really the product of the ruling class and are constructed and encouraged to protect their interests.

A4 Mass culture refers to the products of mass media that encourage people to accept their lot and to concentrate on consumption and trivial entertainment.

***examiner's* note** It is important to focus on neo-Marxist approaches such as those produced by the Frankfurt School, Althusser and Gramsci, as much as on Marx himself.

Marxism (4)

Q1 Why was Marx criticised for being 'over-deterministic'?

Q2 What critique that interactionists make about functionalists can also be applied to Marxism?

Q3 What criticism do postmodernists make of the Marxist view that social class is the main social division in modern societies?

Q4 Why was the neo-Marxist Gramsci critical of Marx?

ANSWERS

A1 Marx was over-deterministic in that he saw the economic system as determining all actions, choices and thought.

A2 Interactionists criticise both Marxists and functionalists for seeing people as the puppets of society — they fail to see that people can exercise real choices and resist the influence of capitalism or society.

A3 There is a range of alternative social divisions in modern societies, including gender, religion, ethnicity and age, just as important as social class.

A4 Gramsci believed the working class could 'resist' ruling-class ideology.

examiner's note Neo-Marxists do not always agree with Karl Marx's original ideas.

Social action theories (1)

Q1 Why is interactionism concerned with symbols?

Q2 What is the self?

Q3 What is a social role?

Q4 What is the role of interaction in society?

ANSWERS

A1 Symbols are a shorthand way that members of society use to interpret the social world, e.g. people may interpret the dress or look of young people as symbolic of delinquency.

A2 The self refers to our ability to see ourselves through the eyes of others.

A3 Social roles refer to the behaviour expected by society of particular statuses, e.g. we expect parents to be loving, or teachers to be professional.

A4 Interaction involves coming together in social groups — e.g. the family, school — and interpreting the meaning of other people's symbolic actions. Interactionists see this process as the basis of society.

examiner's note Social action theory is critical of the structuralist theories of functionalism and Marxism because both fail to see individuals as important.

Social action theories (2)

Q1 Which social action theorist invented the 'dramaturgical' approach?

Q2 How does the dramaturgical approach see social interaction?

Q3 Identify two ways in which structuralist sociologists are critical of social action theories.

Q4 How does Becker's labelling theory apply social interaction to wider social factors such as the distribution of power?

ANSWERS

A1 Erving Goffman.

A2 It sees social interaction as a loosely scripted play in which people, i.e. social actors, interpret their social roles and adapt their behaviour according to the scene — e.g. family, work — that they are 'playing'.

A3
- Social action theory neglects the wider social factors created by the organisation of society, e.g. social class relationships often underpin the contexts in which self, social roles and interaction exist
- It fails to acknowledge or explore power differences between individuals and groups

A4 Becker demonstrated how powerful groups are able symbolically to label less powerful groups as deviant, to benefit themselves.

examiner's note Don't get confused — symbolic interactionism, interpretivism and labelling theory are just alternative names for social action theory.

Feminism (1)

Q1 What do feminists call the system of gender inequalities and male dominance that allegedly exists in modern societies?

Q2 What do liberal feminists blame for reproducing a sexual division of labour in which masculinity is dominant and femininity is subordinate?

Q3 What does Ann Oakley mainly blame for the subordination of women in the labour market?

Q4 What do liberal feminists mean by 'genderquake'?

A1 Patriarchy.

A2 Gender-role socialisation in the family.

A3 The dominance of the mother-housewife role.

A4 A revolution in women's attitudes and behaviour that has made the present generation of young women more focused on educational achievement and careers compared with previous generations.

examiner's note The concept of genderquake is central to understanding women's position in society today.

Feminism (2)

Q1 Identify four reasons why liberal feminists believe that the traditional sexual division of labour is now being dismantled.

Q2 Identify two structural factors that suggest that not all women are equally experiencing a genderquake.

Q3 Identify two workplace-related factors that suggest that women are still facing employment inequalities.

Q4 Which school of feminism suggests that the subordination of women to men is directly linked to their position within capitalist society?

ANSWERS

A1 Any four from:

- Genderquake
- The feminisation of the service sector workforce
- The greater educational success of females
- Greater legal rights, e.g. access to divorce
- Greater equality within marriage

A2

- Ethnicity — some ethnic minority women do not enjoy the same rights and privileges as white women
- Social class — middle-class women have benefitted more than poorer working-class women from genderquake

A3

- Continuing inequality in pay
- The glass ceiling — there is evidence that women are being held back and are consequently under-represented in top jobs

A4 Marxist feminism.

***examiner's* note** It is important to evaluate thoroughly all feminist theories.

Feminism (3)

Q1 In what two ways do women benefit capitalism, according to Benston?

Q2 In what way might women comprise a 'reserve army of labour'?

Q3 Why are Marxist feminists criticised for being tautological?

Q4 Which school of feminism suggests that society is divided into two fundamental gender classes — men and women — whose interests are opposed?

A1 • They provide free domestic labour, which ensures the health and efficiency of male workers

• They reproduce and raise the future labour force at no extra cost to the capitalist class

A2 Women workers are generally less skilled and less likely to be unionised. They are more likely to work part time because of childcare commitments. Consequently, they are more likely to be hired in times of prosperity and the first to be laid off in a recession.

A3 The starting point of their argument — women's exclusion from the workforce and women's responsibility for domestic labour — is also their conclusion.

A4 Radical feminism.

examiner's note Note that Marxist feminism can be used to supplement essays that focus on Marxist or structuralist theories of society.

Feminism (4)

Q1 What do radical feminists mean when they say 'the personal is political'?

Q2 What do black feminists mean when they criticise radical feminists for being ethnocentric?

Q3 Which feminist concludes that patriarchy has evolved from 'private patriarchy' to 'public patriarchy'?

Q4 What is the difference between private and public forms of patriarchy?

ANSWERS

A1 They argue that all personal relationships between men and women are based upon and involve the manipulation of different and unequal amounts of power.

A2 Feminist approaches tend to be based on the experiences of white middle-class women and assume that all women experience patriarchy in the same way.

A3 Sylvia Walby.

A4 Private patriarchy is that found in the domestic sphere, i.e. in the home and family, while public patriarchy is found in public institutions such as the workplace, education and politics.

examiner's note Walby's work is crucial because she points out that there exist different gender regimes that affect groups of women differently.

Feminism (5)

Q1 In what way does Hakim challenge feminist approaches?

Q2 Identify the three work-lifestyle preferences that Hakim claims women adopt in modern Britain.

Q3 How does the work of Ginn et al. challenge Hakim's ideas?

Q4 Which feminist theory claims that sociological enquiry should now focus on 'difference' between femininities rather than on patriarchal inequality?

ANSWERS

A1 Hakim claims that some women rationally choose to interpret work and career as less important than having a family and staying at home to raise children.

A2
- Home-centred, i.e. full-time mothers
- Adaptive — combining work and childcare
- Work-centred — career women

A3 They claim that it is the patriarchal attitudes of employers rather than women's preferences that determine women's position in the labour market.

A4 Postmodern feminism.

examiner's note Do not neglect studies of masculinity and homosexuality.

Late modernity (1)

Q1 What does structuration theory combine?

Q2 How does 'ontological security' contribute to the stability of society, according to Giddens?

Q3 What is 'reflexivity' and how is it linked to 'transformative capacity', according to Giddens?

Q4 Which sociologist suggests that in late modernity we are living in 'risk societies'?

A1 It combines the concepts of social structure and social action.

A2 Ontological security refers to the general belief held by members of society that the natural and social worlds are as they appear to be. This desire for security among members of society helps people to engage in regular patterns of social life.

A3 Reflexivity refers to people's ability to monitor their situation and place in society, and to assess whether they are happy or unhappy. By engaging in reflexivity, people may respond by choosing to change or transform their lives.

A4 Ulrich Beck.

examiner's note Be willing to evaluate the work of Giddens and Beck.

Late modernity (2)

Q1 What does Beck call 'late modernity'?

Q2 What are the central concerns of the culture of late modern societies, according to Beck?

Q3 What does Beck mean by the concept of 'individualisation'?

Q4 What is the cause of the problems of late modernity, according to Beck?

ANSWERS

A1 Advanced or reflective modernisation.

A2 Risk and risk avoidance.

A3 A decline in accepting socially approved roles and an increasing emphasis on making personal choices.

A4 The global political and technological system.

examiner's note It is important to evaluate Beck using the work of Turner and Elliot.

Postmodernism

Q1 What is a meta-narrative?

Q2 How do postmodernist sociologists generally view knowledge?

Q3 Why does the mass of people express a lack of interest in social solidarity and in politics, according to postmodernists such as Baudrillard?

Q4 What are 'sign objects'?

A1 A theory, e.g. functionalism or Marxism, that purports to explain the social world. Postmodernists dismiss such theories as elaborate stories that give comfort to people by helping them believe there is a rational basis to society.

A2
- As a relative concept — no theory is right or wrong, all theories have some relevance
- As a commodity that is socially constructed by the mass media

A3 Because the mass media persuade people via marketing and advertising that conspicuous consumption of brands, designer labels and popular entertainment are more important.

A4 Consumer goods and leisure activities that matter more for the status and image they provide the consumer with than for the article or service itself.

examiner's note Postmodernism can be daunting but don't neglect it if you want to achieve high grades.

Sociology and science (1)

Q1 What is meant by empirical?

Q2 What has been the main influence on positivist research methodology?

Q3 What is the scientific process of collecting evidence to support a hypothesis called?

Q4 Identify four sources of data that positivists regard as highly scientific.

A1 Empirical means 'knowable through our sense' and, in practice, refers to phenomena that can be observed, counted and measured.

A2 The logic and methods of the natural sciences such as chemistry and physics.

A3 The hypothetico-deductive model or approach.

A4
- The social survey (using the questionnaire and/or the structured interview)
- Official statistics (using the comparative method)
- The experiment
- Direct observation (using an observation or content analysis counting schedule)

examiner's note Durkheim's study of suicide should be used to illustrate positivist science in action.

Sociology and science (2)

Q1 Why is Popper so critical of the hypothetico-deductive model?

Q2 According to Popper, why can we never be conclusively right, only conclusively wrong?

Q3 What is the principle of falsification?

Q4 Why is sociology not a science, according to Popper?

ANSWERS

A1 The hypothetico-deductive model aims to collect evidence that supports a hypothesis. Popper argued this was illogical because we can never be conclusively right, only conclusively wrong.

A2 We may collect hundreds of pieces of evidence confirming a hypothesis but we can never be sure that a piece of evidence will not arise to contradict the hypothesis once and for all.

A3 Popper suggests the principle of falsification is more logical, i.e. we should attempt to prove hypotheses wrong, because once something is disproved it can be abandoned and replaced with a fresh conjecture.

A4 Popper believed that sociological research is unscientific because it does not do enough fieldwork to disprove its theories.

examiner's note Be aware that Popper's approach to sociology was shaped by his rather biased anti-Marxism.

Sociology and science (3)

Q1 What is a paradigm and how does it affect choice of scientific method?

Q2 According to Kuhn, why is science slow to progress or evolve?

Q3 According to Kuhn, what is 'scientific revolution'?

Q4 Using Kuhn's concepts, can sociology qualify as a science?

A1 A paradigm is a dominant body of knowledge into which generations of scientists are socialised and which determines the future direction of research and the methods chosen.

A2 The dominant paradigm initially rejects evidence that contradicts its position on any particular issue. Contradictory evidence, which eventually makes the original paradigm untenable, can take decades to build up.

A3 Scientific revolution is the period in which the old paradigm is abandoned and replaced by a new paradigm based on the contradictory evidence into which the next generation of scientists is socialised.

A4 Yes, because some sociologists argue that sociology is characterised by paradigmatic change — the consensus paradigm of functionalism has been overthrown by a conflict paradigm.

examiner's note Kuhn's ideas should be challenged using the work of Sayer.

Sociology and science (4)

Q1 Why does Feyerabend suggest that science is not a rational or logical process?

Q2 According to Kaplan, what is responsible for most scientific breakthroughs?

Q3 What are 'open' and 'closed' sciences, according to Sayer?

Q4 In what ways might sociology be an open science?

ANSWERS

A1 Feyerabend suggests that most scientific research does not follow a rational or logical path because scientific breakthroughs are frequently the result of scientists not obeying the rules.

A2 Inspired guesswork and imagination, luck, accidents etc.

A3 Open sciences speculate about phenomena because hard evidence is difficult to acquire, e.g. seismology, meteorology. Closed sciences involve the collection of data in controlled environments such as laboratories.

A4 Sociology is an open science in that it speculates on the relationship between structures and the behaviour of people.

examiner's note The model of the physical sciences that most people believe is actually misleading.

Sociology and science (5)

Q1 What do feminists mean when they describe both science and sociology as 'malestream'?

Q2 How do postmodernists challenge the idea that rationality, truth and science are all bound together?

Q3 Why do interpretivists reject the idea that social laws shape social action?

Q4 How do interpretivists view the scientific status of sociology?

ANSWERS

A1 Assumptions about knowledge made by science and sociology are based largely on male perceptions and understandings.

A2 Science is merely another meta-narrative like religion and scientists have replaced priests as a source of truth.

A3 Interpretivists argue that human actions are not predictable in the same way as chemicals or plants are because human beings have consciousness and choose how to react. As a result, social action and interpretation are generally unique and not shaped by social laws.

A4 They argue that it really does not matter so long as valid data are collected.

***examiner's* note** There is no simple answer to the question whether or not sociology is a science.

Positivism and quantitative research (1)

Q1 What is a cross-sectional social survey?

Q2 Identify two strengths of longitudinal surveys.

Q3 Identify two weaknesses of longitudinal surveys.

Q4 What two sampling techniques are most commonly used in quantitative research?

ANSWERS

A1 This is the most common type of survey, which collects data at one particular point in time on behaviour and/or beliefs and attitudes using questionnaires and/or interviews.

A2
- Changes over time in behaviour and attitudes can be monitored
- They are high in reliability — all respondents are exposed to the same set of questions

A3
- Drop-out rates can be high, undermining the representativeness of the sample
- Validity can be undermined as the sample becomes over-familiar with the research aims and team

A4 Probability (random) sampling and quota sampling.

***examiner's* note** The major weakness of all surveys is that they cannot easily uncover more complex qualitative feelings and beliefs.

Positivism and quantitative research (2)

Q1 What type of random sampling technique allows the researcher to account for variations in social class, gender etc. in the population being researched?

Q2 If a conventional list-type sampling frame is unavailable, what alternative might be used if the researcher uses a cluster sampling technique?

Q3 Identify two drawbacks of quota sampling.

Q4 What type of research normally involves manipulating one independent variable in order to create change in a dependent variable?

ANSWERS

A1 Stratified random sampling.

A2 A map.

A3 • There is no guarantee that the sample will contain the correct proportion of subgroups (men/women; young/old etc.) normally found in the population

• Researchers tend to choose people they interpret as cooperative etc., and consequently may end up selecting unrepresentative samples

A4 The experiment.

***examiner's* note** Be aware of the reasons why sociologists rarely use the laboratory experiment.

Interpretive sociology and qualitative methods (1)

Q1 What did Weber mean by 'verstehen'?

Q2 Which sociological theories are concerned mainly with exploring meaning and interpretations?

Q3 What is ethnography?

Q4 What is meant by the phrase 'data that speak for themselves'?

ANSWERS

A1 Empathetic understanding, i.e. the researcher should try to see the social world through the eyes of those being researched.

A2 Symbolic interactionism and labelling theory (i.e. social action theories).

A3 The process of observing people in their natural everyday environment.

A4 Data that speak for themselves are in the actual words of those being studied, e.g. quotations, diary extracts.

***examiner's* note** Be detailed in your knowledge about the differences between quantitative and qualitative methods.

Interpretive sociology and qualitative methods (2)

Q1 If positivist research is generally interested in outcomes, what is interpretive research generally interested in?

Q2 What is the main type of ethnographic research method used by sociologists?

Q3 What is meant by 'going native'?

Q4 Why is covert research regarded by some sociologists as ethically suspect?

ANSWERS

A1 The process or dynamics of research, i.e. what is occurring during the research itself.

A2 Participant observation.

A3 Becoming over-friendly with members of the group being observed and losing detachment and objectivity.

A4 The group being observed is deceived by the researcher pretending to be someone else and informed consent is not obtained.

examiner's note Be aware of the differences between the various types of observation technique available to sociologists.

Interpretive sociology and qualitative methods (3)

Q1 What is a focus group?

Q2 Identify two methodological limitations of using focus groups.

Q3 How does snowball sampling work in practice?

Q4 How do interpretive methods generally score for reliability, validity and generalisability?

A1 A group of people, usually fewer than 12 in number, requested to discuss a specific topic while being observed and/or recorded by sociologists.

A2
- Researchers have limited control over the direction of the discussion, which can potentially produce invalid data
- Some people may have strong personalities and dominate the discussion, so undermining the representativeness of the sample

A3 The method involves finding one person who agrees to act as a gatekeeper and to introduce the researcher to a range of contacts who are difficult to access through normal channels, e.g. perhaps because they are engaged in deviant activities.

A4 Very high for validity and very low for reliability and generalisability.

***examiner's* note** Positivist research methods are seen as more scientific than interpretive research methods.

Feminist research methods (1)

Q1 What should be the purpose of feminist sociological research, according to Harding?

Q2 What should be the relationship of the female research subject to the researcher, according to feminist researchers?

Q3 What type of research methods are regarded by feminists as the most effective?

Q4 Identify three reasons why feminists approve of focus groups.

A1 To improve the position of women.

A2 Research should be seen as a joint activity between the researcher and those being studied rather than the researcher presenting as a powerful expert who studies powerless people.

A3 Ethnographic methods that focus on the activities and viewpoints of women in their natural environment.

A4
- They involve women discussing issues in the company of other women
- Differences in power and status are minimised, which allows women to control the direction and content of the discussion
- They give less powerful women a sense of solidarity and power to influence research

examiner's note Feminists believe feminist research methods can open new areas, neglected by male researchers, for discussion.

Feminist research methods (2)

Q1 Which type of interview is the most common tool of research used by feminists?

Q2 Which feminist sociologist pioneered feminist research methods in her study of pregnancy and motherhood 'From here to maternity'?

Q3 What methods were used by Beverley Skeggs when she studied 83 working-class women in her study 'Formations of class and gender'?

Q4 Why might feminist commitment to qualitative research methods be a problem in the long term?

ANSWERS

A1 Unstructured in-depth interviews.

A2 Ann Oakley.

A3 Participant observation at their workplaces and in-depth unstructured interviews.

A4 Quantitative research methods attract more prestige, funding and influence over government policy than qualitative methods.

examiner's note Essays on ethnography or qualitative methods should always attempt to link to feminist research methodology.

Questionnaires, interviews and quantitative approaches

Q1 Identify two differences between a questionnaire and a structured interview.

Q2 What does operationalisation mean?

Q3 How is the concept of generalisability linked to representativeness?

Q4 What is the main difference between reliability and validity?

ANSWERS

A1 • Questionnaires are self-completed whereas an interviewer fills in the questionnaire on behalf of the respondent
• Interviewers can use scripted prompts to collect more information

A2 The process by which a hypothesis and related concepts are put into a form, i.e. questions or categories that can be observed and measured.

A3 If a sample is typical (representative) of a research population, any data collected are probably true of the wider population to which the sample belongs.

A4 Reliability refers to the design of the research method and the need for questionnaires, interviews etc. to be the same as one another. Validity refers to the data collected and whether they measure what the method intended.

examiner's note It is crucial that you understand and are able to illustrate the key concepts of reliability, validity and representativeness.

Interviews and qualitative approaches

Q1 Identify three types of interview in addition to structured and unstructured interviews.

Q2 Why are unstructured interviews regarded as unreliable, according to positivist sociologists?

Q3 What is interviewer effect or bias?

Q4 Why are unstructured interviews thought to produce highly valid data?

A1 Any three from:

- semi-structured interview
- oral history interview
- life history interview
- group interview
- focus group interview

A2 They depend on a unique trusting relationship between the interviewer and interviewee that is impossible to replicate and therefore verify.

A3 The influence of the interviewer on the way the respondent replies. Interviewees may feel threatened by aspects of the interviewer's social status, e.g. their social class, ethnicity, gender, age.

A4 If trust and rapport are established by the interviewer, the meanings and motivations that underpin the behaviour and attitudes of the research subject may be uncovered.

examiner's note Be able to compare in illustrative detail interviews that produce quantitative data with types of interview that produce mainly qualitative data.

Secondary data (1)

Q1 How might positivist sociologists use content analysis to investigate documents and mass media reports?

Q2 What is semiotics?

Q3 What four criteria does Scott identify to judge the usefulness of secondary data?

Q4 What is a 'life document'?

A1 By counting the number of times certain words, themes, advertisements, images, photographs etc. are used.

A2 The study of signs and symbols, and the meanings that underpin them, e.g. the colour red indicates danger in many societies.

A3
- Authenticity
- Credibility
- Representativeness
- Meaning

A4 Life documents include virtually all written, aural and visual material that results from people's personal lives, e.g. diaries, letters, photographs, e-mails.

***examiner's* note** Suicide notes are a type of life document used by interpretivist sociologists such as Atkinson.

Secondary data (2)

Q1 What is the difference between 'hard' and 'soft' statistics?

Q2 Why do interpretivist sociologists claim that crime statistics tell us very little about crime?

Q3 Why is the use of secondary data regarded as relatively unobtrusive research?

Q4 Why might the Census under-represent certain categories of the population?

A1 Hard statistics refer to hard irrefutable facts, e.g. the number of births, that can be interpreted in only one way. Soft statistics involve some interpretation and even political manipulation, and probably tell us more about the groups involved in their collection, e.g. suicide rates say more about the behaviour of coroners than about people who kill themselves.

A2 Crime statistics are the products of the decision of powerful people, e.g. police officers, to record reported crime or to focus resources on detecting a particular type of crime.

A3 It does not generally impact directly on the lives of individuals in the same way as questionnaires, interviews or observation.

A4 Some groups, e.g. refugees, asylum seekers, the homeless and travellers, fail to complete it.

examiner's note Some aspects of the crime and deviance debate, especially criminal statistics and suicide, are really about the methodological usefulness of secondary data.

Multiple methods

Q1 What term originally referred to the use of different indicators in quantitative research in order to overcome any problem if one indicator proved faulty?

Q2 What is 'methodological pluralism' or multi-strategy research?

Q3 In what way is a case study a type of methodological pluralist approach?

Q4 Why are case studies regarded highly by interpretivist sociologists?

A1 Triangulation.

A2 The use of a range of research strategies in order to look at a sociological problem from a variety of angles.

A3 A case study is an in-depth study of the behaviour of an individual, group or institution, using a variety of methods.

A4 Case studies involve an in-depth examination of the motives, attitudes and interpretations of research subjects in order to understand their version of social reality. The qualitative data generated are thought to be high in validity.

examiner's note Some of the classic sociological studies, e.g. Paul Willis's 'Learning to Labour', are in fact case studies.

Value freedom (1)

Q1 Why did Comte call sociology the 'science of society'?

Q2 What is meant by value freedom?

Q3 What criticism, in regard to funding, is often made of the notion of value freedom?

Q4 What is the relationship between positivism and value freedom?

ANSWERS

A1 Comte believed that sociologists were social engineers who could use their scientific abilities to create a better society.

A2 Value freedom refers to the ability of sociologists to be objective, i.e. to avoid imposing their own prejudices and opinions on the research process and findings.

A3 Sociologists sometimes receive their funding from powerful interests such as governments or businesses and, consequently, may avoid producing findings that criticise social policy or particular business practices.

A4 Generally positivists believe that the scientific status of sociology depends on sociologists being disinterested and value-free champions of truth.

examiner's note Some positivists believe that they do not have to take responsibility for how their sociological data are used by politicians and social policy-makers.

Value freedom (2)

Q1 What is meant by the observation that value freedom is impossible because data collection is a social process?

Q2 What do postmodernists believe in regard to scientific and value-free knowledge and truth?

Q3 What is Gouldner's critique of value freedom?

Q4 How might value freedom be undermined by sociologists' career trajectories?

ANSWERS

A1 Value freedom is impossible because people use their value systems to make sense of social research and to shape how they are going to respond to a questionnaire, interview or observation.

A2 Postmodernists believe that there is no such thing as objective absolute truth and that all knowledge has relatively equal value.

A3 Gouldner believes that the decision to pursue particular types of research tends to reflect the dominant assumptions or values of a particular society or historical period.

A4 Sociologists have personal ambitions and career goals, which might influence what they choose to study, their research methods and their findings.

***examiner's* note** Most sociologists now accept that value freedom is extremely difficult to achieve — many researchers now include a discussion of how their own values have impacted on their research.

Value freedom (3)

Q1 Why is Gomm critical of the idea of value freedom?

Q2 According to radical sociologists such as Marxists, what is the purpose of social research?

Q3 Why do feminist sociologists see sociological research as value laden?

Q4 Can sociological research ever be value free?

ANSWERS

A1 Gomm argues that value freedom is merely a means by which some sociologists can avoid taking responsibility for the way their research findings are used by governments.

A2 To change society or the social conditions of groups that are experiencing inequality, powerlessness, exploitation and oppression, such as the poor, ethnic minorities and women.

A3 Because it is malestream, i.e. it reflects patriarchal values.

A4 Sociologists can attempt to ensure that personal values and bias do not shape the outcome of their research, although reflexivity will usually acknowledge that bias cannot be totally avoided.

***examiner's* note** Critical accounts such as Marxism and feminism have openly practised a form of value-laden sociology aimed at changing society for the better.

Sociology and social policy (1)

Q1 What is social policy?

Q2 Identify four links that Giddens makes between sociology and social policy.

Q3 Give two examples of cultural differences that sociology has made social policy-makers more aware of.

Q4 What is the difference between a 'social' problem and a 'sociological' problem?

ANSWERS

A1 Government policies that are aimed at solving social problems.

A2
- Sociology results in clearer understanding of social situations, e.g. the reasons for poverty
- Sociology raises awareness of cultural differences
- Sociology can assess the impact of social policies
- Sociology encourages people to increase their self-knowledge by comparing their experiences with others

A3 Disability; homosexuality; ethnicities; religions; etc.

A4 A social problem usually impacts negatively on a society, e.g. divorce, crime, poverty, and requires social policy to resolve it. A sociological problem is an academic or theoretical problem focused on social processes or phenomena such as why we live in nuclear families.

examiner's note Some sociologists believe that the relationship between sociology and social policy is one-sided in that sociology has been colonised by governments that have tamed its radical instincts.

Sociology and social policy (2)

Q1 How do postmodernists such as Bauman view the relationship between sociology and social policy?

Q2 Identify four reasons why social policy-makers may fail to respond to sociological findings.

Q3 Why is Walters critical of the relationship between sociologists and governments?

Q4 Why does democracy limit what social change sociologists and social policy-makers can bring about?

A1 They argue that sociology has no contribution to make to social policy because society is not orderly and manageable.

A2
- The group being studied is not powerful enough
- Social policy is limited by lack of funds
- There may be too much opposition to social policy from vested interests
- Governments may be uncommitted to social change

A3 He argues that sociological research into crime is too dependent on government funding, which undermines the objectivity of the research.

A4 Democracy in the UK means that governments take power for only a limited period. They may consequently be reluctant to force through dramatic change for fear of alienating their voters.

examiner's note There is no agreement among sociologists about whether sociologists should encourage social policy-makers to use sociological evidence to bring about positive social change.

H. Parker: *View from the Boys* (1993)

Parker studied a group of young delinquent males in Liverpool, using participant observation. He was able to blend in with them because he was in his early twenties and had an untidy and informal dress sense. He also impressed them with his ability at swearing and football. He gained their trust by demonstrating his loyalty to them by passing various 'tests', including acting as a lookout while they broke into cars, receiving stolen goods and spending his leisure time drinking heavily with them. Towards the end of the study, when the 'Boys' were being prosecuted for their crimes, they turned to him for support and advice.

Evaluation of Parker

- This was an ethnographic study — Parker spent all his free time with members of the subculture in their own environment
- Parker's personal characteristics eased his access into the subculture and established the trust and rapport required to produce highly valid data
- We can never be sure whether the boys' behaviour was not the result of Parker's presence: they may have exaggerated their behaviour in order to show off to him
- Parker has been accused of losing his objectivity and 'going native'
- Parker has been accused of unethical behaviour in that he engaged in criminal behaviour

D. J. Smith and J. Bradshaw: *Gang Membership and Teenage Offending* (2005)

The authors carried out a longitudinal research study into why teenagers joined gangs and to document what types of crime gang members committed. Their research focused on 23 state secondary schools, eight independent schools and nine special schools. Taking a multi-strategy approach, they asked participants to complete self-report questionnaires focused on gang membership and crimes committed. They then carried out semi-structured interviews with a subsample to obtain more in-depth data, and asked teachers and parents to complete questionnaires, as well as examining secondary data in the form of social work reports and documents from juvenile courts.

EVALUATION

Evaluation of Smith and Bradshaw

- The multi-strategy approach collected both quantitative and qualitative data in both primary and secondary forms
- The pluralistic nature of the research produced a multi-angled overview of the problem
- All participants were exposed to the same stimulus in terms of the questions and interviews, so reliability was high
- Self-reports can produce invalid data in that respondents may not respond honestly to questions about criminal or deviant behaviour because they are suspicious of the motives of the researcher or they fear punishment
- The questionnaires and interviews are written by adult researchers and may miss out crucial questions that give insight into how young people see the world
- It is doubtful whether the secondary data used can give insight into the motives, feelings and interpretations of the teenagers being studied, because of the secondhand nature of these data

The British Crime Survey

The British Crime Survey conducted by the Home Office is done annually and used by the government in devising policies on crime. The 2008 survey carried out 46,983 face-to-face interviews with a sample of people aged 16 and over living in private households in England and Wales, using laptops.

This computer-assisted self-interviewing aims to increase the validity of the data by assuring respondents of anonymity. The sample is randomly selected from the Postcode Address File and is designed to be a nationally representative sample in order to generalise to the country as a whole. The overall response rate in 2008 was 76%.

Evaluation of the British Crime Survey

- The BCS is thought to provide a valid reflection of the extent of household and personal crime because it asks about crimes not reported to the police and not recorded in the crime statistics
- It is the most reliable measure of national trends over time
- The response rate is reasonably high
- The survey is thought to be highly reliable in that the sample is exposed to the same set of questions annually
- Computer-assisted interviewing improves the validity of the data because it ensures confidentiality
- The types of questions asked are limited by the nature of crime, i.e. it cannot ask about serious crimes, crimes against businesses or corporate crimes, which reduces validity
- People's responses depend on memory, which can be faulty and partial
- Is it ethical to ask people to relive the trauma of crime?

S. Jones: *Partners in Crime* (2008)

This study aimed to find out whether increased female offending was the result of choice or whether women were influenced by men. The sample comprised women who had been found guilty of an offence for which they had been charged jointly with a male.

Jones asked women in one prison to volunteer to be interviewed and 50 agreed to take part. He carried out semi-structured interviews focused on their social backgrounds and their relationship with their male co-defendant. All interviews were tape-recorded and carried out in private.

Evaluation of Jones

- Semi-structured interviews are likely to have produced a combination of quantitative and qualitative data
- Qualitative questions may have produced highly valid 'data that speak for themselves', i.e. quotations from the women that give sociologists insight into their motives and how they interpret the social world they inhabit
- Jones's emphasis on privacy may have increased the women's trust in the research and encouraged them to open up in ways not accessible through questionnaires
- Tape-recording interviews (with the permission of respondents) can increase validity because the interviewer is not distracted by taking notes
- Women from just one prison may not have been very representative of female offenders in the UK
- The women volunteered to take part in the research; those who did not volunteer might have had different experiences

L. Humphreys: *Tearoom Trade* (1970)

This study was a covert participant observation of homosexual sexual encounters in public toilets (known as tearooms) carried out in the USA in the 1960s. Humphreys, a heterosexual sociologist, wanted to gain entry to a deviant subculture. Aware that homosexuals then were wary of sociologists and research, he went under cover as a 'voyeur watchqueen' (a recognisable role in the gay community), referring to gay men who derived pleasure from watching the homosexual behaviour of others, while keeping an eye out for the police. Consequently, he was able to move around the 'tearoom' at will without being expected to take part in any sexual activity.

Evaluation of Humphreys

- Humphreys' data were highly valid because the people he was observing assumed he was a peer and consequently did not think about covering up their behaviour
- His research was covert so it is unlikely that his presence was the cause of the behaviour he observed
- At one stage, Humphreys was arrested and jailed, further increasing his credibility with the gay men he was observing, which probably added to the validity of his data
- Humphreys' research could be described as unethical because he deceived his research group and did not ask for their informed consent
- The study cannot be viewed as statistically representative
- Humphreys justified his unethical position by suggesting that this was a study of police attitudes rather than homosexuality: he wanted police officers to be more sensitive and understanding towards homosexual behaviour

P. Waddington et al.: *The Police and Stop and Search* (2004)

Waddington et al. were interested in why it is accepted that members of ethnic minority groups are unfairly stopped.

Their research in Slough and Reading used a multi-strategy approach. First, they examined CCTV footage in order directly to observe police at work on the streets. Second, they analysed secondary data in detail (official police records of stop and search). Third, they interviewed police officers about their stop and search activities.

They concluded that police stop and searches in the areas researched reflected the composition of people out on the streets, especially in the evenings, rather than any racial bias.

Evaluation of Waddington et al.

- Multi-strategy approaches collect both quantitative and qualitative data in both primary and secondary forms
- Watching CCTV footage does not provide qualitative insight into the reasons for stopping members of particular ethnic groups
- Interviewing police officers may give qualitative insight into their reasons for stopping suspects
- Some police officers may not be aware that they are stopping members of some ethnic groups more often than others because they subconsciously subscribe to racial stereotyping
- Most police officers are aware of the negative connotations of racism and consequently would deny this is the basis of their actions

H. Parker et al.: *Illegal Leisure* (1998)

Parker et al. conducted the North West Longitudinal Study, which involved following several hundred young people aged 14 to 18 for a period of 5 years. The aim was to see how average young people growing up in the 1990s dealt with the easy availability of alcohol and drugs.

The main research strategy was a self-report questionnaire sent out to hundreds of teenagers by post, although some were administered by researchers in night clubs. The researchers attempted to ensure that the sample who participated in the research was representative of young people in the North West in terms of gender, class and ethnicity.

Evaluation of Parker et al.

- The study was able to document changes over time in both attitudes and behaviour
- The size of the sample and the attempts made at representativeness meant that the results of the study could be generalised to other similar groups in the North West
- Questionnaires are usually reliable because all respondents are exposed to the same questions
- Such questions produce a great deal of quantitative data that can be used to compare for correlations
- Self-report questionnaires on deviant behaviour such as drug use are notorious for producing invalid data because teenagers may exaggerate or distort reports about their behaviour
- The drop-out rate for samples in longitudinal behaviour can undermine their representativeness, e.g. this study lost a disproportionate number of working-class and Asian respondents

The Offending, Crime and Justice Survey (2008)

This nationally representative longitudinal self-report survey asked young people in England and Wales about their attitudes and experiences of offending. Its main aim was to discover the extent of offending, antisocial behaviour and drug use among young people aged 10 to 25.

From the Postcode Address File sampling frame, 5,000 young people were chosen to take part in an hour-long highly structured interview, in which questions were read from a laptop and the answer inputted by the interviewer. Delicate questions were managed by giving the sample a laptop with headphones so the sample could listen to the questions and answer in private.

EVALUATION

Evaluation of the Offending Crime and Justice Survey

- The research design produced valid qualitative data because respondents were put at the centre of the research experience, i.e. the technology was geared towards ensuring confidentiality and therefore trust
- Reliability was high because a large number of people were subjected to the same questions
- The sample was large and nationally representative, which means data could be generalised to other young people across the country who shared similar characteristics
- The data could be compared each year in order to document changing attitudes and patterns of offending of young people as they got older
- Self-report questionnaires rarely provide data on serious crime
- Respondents may react to questions about deviance in various invalid ways, e.g. exaggeration, partiality, deception
- The random nature of the sampling method is unlikely to include significant numbers of criminal young people